greenhouse of
graves

Eloise McGifford

BookLeaf Publishing

India | USA | UK

Presentation by *BookLeaf Publishing*

Web: www.bookleafpub.com

E-mail: info@bookleafpub.com

ISBN : 9789357447744

First edition 2021

DEDICATION

To a someone full of rebellion and fire, who shared it with me.

To another who told me to never stop writing and to always read.

Thanks you Erin and Ash

ACKNOWLEDGEMENT

Thanks for a brilliant artist for designing my cover!

odeur de forêt.

Such a lovely piece of art,
wandering aimless while the world is spinning.
Pine trees swimming in the dead brush around
them.
slowly they turn their leaves to the stars.
pondering just where the hell they are,
for they want a place.

The odeur de forêt is sweet,
sweeter then the sound of love,
so much sweetness then the sound of woe.
Only the flowers know.
How can something so small fill a heart with
more hope?
They have relinquished a power of folly.
never could they see
the sweet smell is only filled with melancholy.

Without inviting an ache,
you breath it in.
Slowly the trees are spinning
everything is captured and being devoured.
The vast rivers have a history,
you'll own the dripping water.
The Moon only sees a pity.

"You were so pretty"

a ghost that isn't dead

You'll end up as words,
I've tricked you.
I'm a hidden poet
you're left in these lines for eternity.
You'll be read on a whim,
you won't be laughing at her wit now.
I'll see this ghost waiting for the end on time.

I use to imagine you,
Standing with me.
Trembled alone.

She sleeps with a ghost
Making me moan
with the frightened unknown
a cold frozen hurt.
Hot water streams
But feels chilling.
Implosions of burning skin.

Don't hearts have guards?
Your words are drowning out of your mouth,

Ripping at a poets feet.
Really life fades,
They score, she is disappearing unafraid

You've made my body a crime
my portrait is a chalk outline.
Someone is destined to die
by a poet or ghost.
Because the poet fell in love
With a cruel situation.

potions of colour

I remember when.
When my heart was soft and blameless
colour is slipping
dripping
flowing and
towing my emotions
every feeling is taking control
running colours down your walls.
Humans leak colour,
Blue are tears.
Worry is purple.
Yellow is happiness
And warning, Hurry!
Dears envy is green.
Like is bleak
We always focus on one colour,
Take in
Red anger
And brown bruises
Touch her
My
Our
Skin.
All the colours leak.
Past a point to seek the meaning.

Let them pour,
They mix where they are unrecognizable.
Smell them in the air.
Wish them farewell.
Emotions are a spell,
Pour the potions down your walls
Let them drift and pool.
Fill the hollow heart you have.

to be in possession of a room

White walls,
Small   lights
unread books
the calm air is full of coldness.
Not in the way or sadness but as if it is trying to
protect.
Outgrown hair waiting to be cut, thinning edges
containing the last memory of blushed dye
a shivering cup of tea
or was it coffee?
Misplaced recollection
Consigned to oblivion.
White walls see all,
Colour is blotted out, to begin anew.
Dreams are only detected by the stars.
stars shine
moon shine
sun shine
this room observed it all,
catches a glimpse of
uneaten dinners.
lost glasses.

dried flowers
was it the wish?
or was the greenhouse abandoned?
It slipped one's mind,
Whoever is to be in possession of this room.
Where they willing to come back to a dead end?
Or a room they call home.

Coffee with the widow maker

Is there a bookshop close by?
I mentioned to the sky.
Death will never die.
Where can one sit with a cup of death?
I can take a deep breath
And read
Commit the deed in a simple café.

To join with the widow maker,
Maybe eat a jam tart.
Sweet things numb the pain,
Kind words on the sunlit train.
I wander in my brain.
You sit perplexed at what nature can do.

"A failure to thrive"
Thy cannot maintain
To obtain death.

Human   evolution,
To better the species.

We want them to illumine our world.
I will write a letter
"death isn't a concept"
You'll see a white flash
That can disappear the memories in a night.
As you lay to rest for centuries.

my greenhouse

In a peaceful garden I watch.
Flowers are growing up my back
Hanging over my shoulders.
I feel the thorns pinning me down.

flowers are growing up my back
girls are in my head
they are just trying to devour
making the dead.

flowers are growing up my back.
I standing in a greenhouse
No longer it has possession.
Waiting for you to grow,
Grow my safety blanket
Make me feel whole,
But I've entrusted too much
Upset flowers do not want to bloom
Ferns are growing over my fingers.
cut with shattered class
conceals the broken red

flowers are growing up my back.
Clouds are in the sky,
My flowers are wilting

And tilting.

A warning sign has appeared on a garden.
"do no enter,
toxic flowers"
I've got no home for my flowers.
They are growing up my back,
Wandering down my spine
I try to whine.
They are seeping in my blood line,
Already in my head, a lifeline

In my future I can only see windows
Viewing a gardens new aloneness. abandonment.
Vines winding down my arms.
Pick a broken name,
Called back.
"come home"
Twisting my words.
A garden filled with clarity
A distinctly sharp outline of what is fenced
won't stay long,
the phone never stops ringing in rain.

My green house is no longer here
At the center of a story.
Where light was eaten,
Nothing could grow.
coldness in the greenhouse,

Bloodless in the greenhouse.
Pushing up daisies.
And I've gone to meet the maker.

Powder Pierrot

A wholesome ideal,
watch them change a cherry figure.
Puffed on the comers,
a ruff on a neck pumping with blood.

Seen as a fool,
struggles with being a poster child.
comes only to seek love,
but humans see him as painted insecurity.
he was acquainted with being a puppet,
when unmasked he was no longer charming
but his suffering is uncovered.
harming only our view.

His only friend is the moon,
our only sight at night.
we are connected,
we are bathed with the demeaning,
graved with it white light,
we see our gloom,
we steal our own room.
to hear a fearful voice,
"you emblem suffering"

with the only words you can muster

"am I pierrot now, destined to be an unsuccessful
lover?"
"I'll pity you, but you've always been my
audience,
I never leave, forever in history.
because you've been made-up"

A poet's flowers

A poet eats all the sunflowers,
the light within them kill the grief.
Poets love spring because it is a decoy.
watching the flowers are all darkly coloured,
when you look up to the sky
turning to the night,
full of wit
having the illogical changes of a mind.

A poet writes about their whimsicality,
they cannot be denied.
their mind willing wanders to this.
The sky has turn bright,
with no delight it.
this gift hurts their flowers.

flowers grow,
an orchard in their palm.
this brightness flows.
throws the breeze,
these bring the seeds.

But you've been deceived,
she was never a poet

or had flowers,
just stood out
waited for something whole
for control
for anything to stop them wilting.
don't tell her that she is the poison,
that she ate.
so she doesn't need to wait to feel the cold
and it's numbness take hold.

forget-me-nots are growing

I like watching you,
I'll forever ponder the way you hum,
Or the way you try to teach the stars.
They are so far.
I'm curious who you take me for,
Am I a bore?
It that I'm looked at as a chore?

Late at night,
I feel you whisper,
They tingle my toes,
Help we watch the world grow.
But I can't help but wonder,
If you really know
How much you toll,
And overthrow,
Every feeling I know.
Same flush of longing
To keep going.
But stop growing

you're someone I don't know,
A sweet smell of a flower that don't grow,
I seemingly died long ago.
On death row,
Beside someone who is a no go

Jealousy of missing

pure peppermint and milky coffee.
you i fear,
is it your actions? or your thoughts?
oh what? an internal monologue
never did I think, your sweet sugar would taste
so much like death,
a sour taste in the back of my throat.
and I'm still awaiting for a spoonful of
fellowship,
and I taste the pull
of the child inside
it cried "hugs have limitations,
kisses form a tragedy,
that's what Shakespeare read".
dead, in my head,
a past full of vast rainfalls of
pain.

a waiting game,
shame in my brain,
eye pour rain,
crystal clear windows on the train, while I run.

A girl in-between,

I am little,
she is like unmatched socks,
honey and rice
sad smiles
out of order.
are criminal,
as this is a subliminal conscious perception

playing in the attic
of yourself

you've stepped in this room before,
can you figure it out?
You watched the stars tease you,
the moon light peering through.

You swam in tears in this room over small
issues,
can you figure it out?
You used it a place to hide,
you were so frightened of your head
you couldn't feel your feet on the ground.

you've sat in here and wondered of your life,
can you figure it out?
wanting you boil your existence down to nothing
feeling low and like each blow will cause you to
disappear.

you can't figure it out.
you're in so much doubt,
you touch your cheeks

it leeks, because you've realized what this room
is.
its in the corner of your brain no one talks about,
the dark part;
which explores your heart.
they don't give you a reason not to visit,
your spirit is closed off.

misplaced fish

deep dark rivers flow
and go
past the spaces
these are vast
covered in glass
and here in the underpass,
we have misplaced fish
dashed with a wish.

Missing the morning sun,
kissing the early dew.
part of the policy
of the paper you find.
you see as you dart,
"would you mind, the misplaced fish"

misplaced fish
based in your dish,
they are spaced
and raced to the unknown
undergrown full of leaves,
you perceive these misplaced
how these people grieve,
when misplaced you says "please"

the stars

have you ever wondered;
when you look out on the stars
and count each one and pondered,
out outside of us, their is someone reading a
book.
Wait stay a minutes longer and wander;
someone is pleading to be loved,
but sitting with a monster.

have you ever looked at the moon,
thinking someone outside in the world
is watching
the same thing.
but they are alone
or sitting with a ghost
that is waiting with the grasses.

Someone hating the flowers, but watching the
moon,
or is a sweet girl breaking the rules of what?
or is she songwriting and taking control.
oh honestly we cannot predict,
or write a script
for our own mind,
who is the real mastermind

behind what happens?

would death?

Are you having fun tearing me apart?
tiny pricks by a little dart,
empty words tumble out of my mouth,
my aches shutter into a thousand little pieces,
and it hurts,
it hurts.
It hurts so bad.
but instead of telling him,
I let a laugh roll out of my lungs,
before a gasp of tears come
because little do you know.
I've never felt alone,
I just want to be saved by him.
I'm a weakened package,
intimate things make me feel hyper alone.
surviving was easy when I didn't want to.
It's a simple biological response,
to the world burning around me.
I am so afraid,
I'm simply dazed and
unfazed.
because I am so alone.

tomorrow's weather

I'll inform the sky
trees cry
flowers petals untie
pollen is in great supply
grey clouds are nearby
sunlight passes by.

Drops from the sky,
hops from the moon,
like an open wound.
It predicted midafternoon,
inflicted by tomorrow's weather

the garden in dew
pardon the rain,
it wants to be drained
and arranged in tomorrows weather.

smell the deep fog,
the Death knell
of a period to undress,
to remove the weak
and let the sky reek,
as rain must leak
in tomorrows weather

drinking a poet

drink a poet's soul,
withhold underwater.
you'll hold my hand,
while you drown my words;
feeding poetry within
watch out for the ink on your skin,
it's a sin.

drink a poet's soul,
did you wish for your lungs to be still?
but as you lie still,
words are forming in the captions.
you're drunk in emotion.

suddenly you find yourself
holding a breath,
writing is picturesque
and pressed in skin
as if you're sin.
Alas let the poet begin,
break in your lips
to spin words
to cut in, others souls

hearts will stop

Hearts are a fucked-up thing.
The first time it is heard it cannot break,
The tump, tatta, thump.
A heart though can shatter quick
A bump, a word, a deed,
Pain found, clouding the truth.
Touched gentle but never softly
Skin brushed up against yours.

Hope but intensely felt fear
Sprung up but why?
Mistaking
Or taken as it is pure innocents' excitement.
Feelings tingle and hearing mumbles
Through
Weaken phrases
"please" "oh" "mercy"

Spring from a stumble, toil and so much trouble
What has gone wrong?
It is okay, it is right
I'm not uptight
But please stop despite saying

"I'm being honest, it is perfect"
 I'm full of so much fright
Stop
My heart has no delight.
Rising thumping and bumping
Shattering and pattering.

I am still here, am I?
It feels wrong
Hot water hits like darts calming me
Like a gun,
I am for slaughter,
I've fought her…
The monster inside
Returns to fear.
Show me, tell me, ask me, help me,
Write me, paint me, hug me.
Please.

Anything, my heart is going to break,
Like a mistake
Your mistake.
I hold only that

A night of teenage dreams

Sweet joy looked upon, watching, waiting hating
Salty swear or tears, smeared lipstick tumbling
hair cascading.
Sounds of normality and divergence.
Soft skin gentle running
Tip, tap, tapping
Crowding, counting, clouding
Thoughts
Lingering perfumes of pleasure
Passionate nights
Measure of sadness
Star lights sparkle.
Beats move through your bones,
Carelessly making you feel whole
taking control.
Heart beats
Tears streams.
A quite dance to something
That is a teenage dream

Red is bittersweet

an old cottage,
a fire warm,
a world lit by
moon.
stars.
fright.
dusted by fallen memories.
the sky holds on to them,
the chilled,
and in the dim light
you'll weep in the snow,
Tarnished of past fates.

These patterns stay inhabited in the snow,
he will watch you in evanescent.
without warning you'll feel the water trickle
down,
the snow is melting
its getting hotter in your head,
you're awaking the dead
frozen memories.
you are left.

and Mr Moon
high in the sky turns to your fear

"you've been forgotten, lets make that clear"

While you fade into the cold,
the haunting melancholia that dominates what
you've been told,
watches you become red.
feels the anger of the red.
see your passion of the red.
the heat of the red.
you're wet with something red.
but reeks of the dead

the lot

Out here in the cold,
bodies mold,
form a clump
to feel any warm.
Let them stay whole?

a kind friend has given you flowers!
You should spend the weekend,
its no longer a dead end;
you should mend your old love
above the ground!

It's really quite a shame,
some say a pity.
You two can no longer be witty,
spend days in the windy city
because they are above.

Never their pain,
they take their rain
to visit you
while your blood drains
into the grounds veins.

I wonder if they see,

how it's an enormous façade
that will be laid
as people fade.
To trade
and aid in how a person deals die

Blanket flowers

They grow small,
some plant them for medicine
other for a carpet of colour
For someone to pick
to charm.
Little girls wander lonely
and breath in the trees
in the breeze
fluttering and dancing
like honeybees.

she is a flower,
the sun
and their bloom.
She decorates a room,
with a blanket flowers.

On a sun kissed day,
in a special town,
she has turned to a blanket of flowers.
An unknown garden, they say
where children play
a bouquet of misplaced lilies and roses
laced and displaced
Wishing they could keep smelling sweet

in this heat.

Somehow they find something they don't see,
a special treasure
a girl growing with the flowers,
as she towers
the dark rose red,
of her death bed.